Trans

Trans

Hilda Raz

Wesleyan University Press
Middletown, Connecticut

Published by
Wesleyan
University Press,
Middletown,
CT 06549
© 2001 by Hilda Raz
All rights reserved.
Printed in the
United States of
America.
Designed by
Dika Eckersley.
Set in Quadraat by
B. Williams &
Associates.
5 4 3 2 1   CIP data
appear at the back
of the book

for Aaron Link

Trans-, prefix. The Latin preposition trans, across, to or on the farther side of, beyond, over, . . . beyond the boundary or frontier . . . to look through, to transcend, to transcribe . . . to hand over, to lead across . . . a crossing.

In English . . . the chief uses are as follows:

1. With the sense across, through, over, to or on the other side, beyond . . . from one person, state, or thing to another.

2. In verbs, as in *transboard, transearth, transfashion, tranship, trans-shape, transtime.*

3. In adjectives with the sense across, crossing or on the other side of

4. With the sense beyond, surpassing, transcending.

Oxford English Dictionary

What Survives

Who says that all must vanish?
Who knows, perhaps the flight
of the bird you wound remains,
and perhaps flowers survive
caresses in us, in their ground.

It isn't the gesture that lasts,
but it dresses you again in gold
armor – from breast to knees –
and the battle was so pure
an Angel wears it after you.

Rainer Maria Rilke, translated by J. B. Leichman

Contents

1. With the sense across,
   through, over, to or on
   the other side, beyond
   . . . from one person,
   state, or thing to
   another

Avoidance

Today I'd like to write about epistemology or quarks, the habits of the leech – so useful in medical treatment, a horror in the pond – the growth and development of the precious embryo, attended, monitored until the radiance and blood of birth, the crash of hardwood cultivated for lumber, delight as the oak falls through undergrowth, the whine of the saw, the layers peeling off into fans, falling through their own fragrance to muslin pallets, dust in the chilly air raising a grit halo – or the burble coffee falls from into the cup as you pour a refill – all paid for, earned, the morning deserved, the back seat of the car piled with book bags, their bright canvas a rainbow of good work done, evening hours invested, the lucky deposit on cabins in the Maine woods, moose, ponds, gravel paths and in the near distance the salt, the crash of an ocean contained by its verge of rock.

So consider the weight of the child in his mother's arms, the reds and yellows of the photos, the leisurely flow of language, no compression, nothing packed or forced, no attempt to move in, no microcosm/macrocosm, no abstractions tied into the concrete, no natural paths sealed over to retain or meander, no wretched friends to accompany on their final walks.

Consider the tick, then, veinless, says the biologist in the deep voice of the woman he was, useful as a figure for survival, researchers crush them in vises under tons of pressure, in sealed hermetic chambers devoid of air, pumped free of all essentials – and the tick scurries out, alive, cheerful, the size of a grape.

We all shudder, down to the last woman at this table of learning, old friends all, colleagues.

What to make of our profiles: age, religious preference, marital history, hobbies, our experience with Hale-Bopp, did we see the comet at all, note its tail as . . . what?

What Do You Want?

Only when I write do I feel well. Then I forget all of
life's vexations, all its sufferings, then I am wrapped
in thought and am happy.

Kierkegaard's journal, 1847

Well, to be honest, a lace blanket, holes
fabricated as patter, light through tapping out
hello and a window wide enough to hold it all up.
A filigree shirt opaque at navel and breast.
A rosewood trivet of openwork made
on the lathe to support a column, to support us.
Oh, silly configurations, a pile of light.

The smell of cold air, your skin as you crawl in
the pull of the tooth leaving its socket
your cheek in my palm
our knees firm in their tough ligaments
click of rotating ankle, toes sucking mud
boots and woolen socks hard from the wash.
Your birth.

The end of it.

Drought: Teaching, Benedict, Nebraska

Merce says, it don't do to get too attached to any of 'em,
her grandson for example, he's four – you might lose them.

In 1972 she come home from town, some fool party
or other, to find her husband lying on the floor
under the kitchen table. You can't hide from me,
she said, I can see your feet. But he didn't move.

Nothing worse than that except the tornado
come right after, her sisters driving out of town
after dropping her off on the porch, their car stuck,
must have been a swirl in the middle of that wind,
the vacuum, that kept them stock-still though the tires rolled,
she could see it, until they drove loose inches only farther south,
and got away. Meantime she called Mama two houses down.

When the neighbor seen Ma running in the road, she come too.
Then the kids from the farm, and Judy from York, her girl
just back from the hospital with tonsils, wrapped up in a quilt
(like the doctor said). We all went into the storm cellar
and Juddy, my oldest, insisted on pushing up the door
just as the funnel passed so his boys could see it go
– David still on the kitchen floor, they wouldn't let me touch him
before the doctor – and all of us there for half an hour
till it passed, the sheriff's men stationed one at each corner
of the section to watch for the ambulance.

Later on the porch with the family around, all afternoon I leaned
over the railing and heaved and gagged – just nerves, was all it was.
I hope I don't have to go through that again,
but that's what a life's for, I guess, they say the Lord
don't put more on a soul than she can bear.

Merce fills my cup with good Swede coffee, starts the breakfast
     dishes.
She's eighty and I'm just up from an operation, come from Lincoln
to teach my first poetry writing class this spring.
The gray sky promises rain and believe me, we need it.
Drink up, she says. And I do.

Tough

says Mom, that's tough. My list
of near escapes, excuses for late
homework, curfews, periods.
Really, Mom, I say, I can't.
Tough luck. Tough turkey.
I do it, wash the car, run
to the store, shine my shoes,
finish my math, finish my
Latin – ad astra per aspera –
brush my teeth. Tough it out,
the bad back, the alterations,
the droops and tucks, the altercations,
war, the political party, mayhem, tough
titty, tough luck, tough chance. Too bad.

The tough steak breaks down
in a marinade of vinegar and spices
the muscles give way, acid a broth
of change, flavor. Ah, but under teeth
delicious resistance.

Melts in the mouth
says Aunt Anne
grinning at us,
three nieces in lawn dresses
eating creme puffs in a hot New York deli.

Names My Mother Knew

Hinda for Hilda: her mother
and me, and also the cousin
with freckles, and the red-haired
pixie we visited by boat
the summer her mother, *Vivian*,
was pregnant with *Peter.*

Skeezix, her name for my embryonic
brother, awash and safe in her
tough interior; then *Jimmy*,
the toddler; *James*, the professor,
and graveside, his full measure,
Barton James, ash, buried
again, perfectly safe.

Aaron, her daddy, our Papa;
and *Frank*, from childhood
her beloved; her sisters
Anne, Jane, Phyllis, and the *Dolly*
she was; *David*, her brother.

The nicknames she called us:
Shepsalie, little sheep, for me
and the habit before sleep
of the catalogue of the loved ones
called to God's attention.

Rosetta, who helped her clean
Harvard Street; *George*, who set the screens,
washed windows, scared us with his false teeth.
Dr. Wollans, who diagnosed mumps;
Dr. Kerchel, who straightened teeth;
Mr. Thumb who lived in my mouth.
She whispered his name before
she pulled him out.

Mr. Eastman's house; *Palmyra,*
the ice cream place; *Canandaigua*
for hot dogs and hamburgs, onion rings.
Genesseo Hospital where we were born.
Nana she was to her grandchildren.
Devorah, her Hebrew name.

Parkinson's patient 723 in the medical study.
West End Lane, her Hampstead address; the *Flandre,*
a ship she sailed on: lost
with the rest: her favorite novels
all foxed, gone.

Houses

Something about rage
about women merged with houses
their flesh loosening over emerging bones.
Something about never, no never
able to refuse, to choose this life
or that, always bent over the sweet flesh
of our small ones, making shade for fragile skin
how much our palms love to smooth hair back
kiss the nape under the braid, the damp forehead
under the baseball cap, brush palms over flushed cheeks,
the little winged backs, tuck curls under the elastic brim.

She asks each morning to be remembered to God
in her 100th year, at the same time
wondering why in her chest the ta-dum,
ta-dum goes on. Each night she councils
her heart to stop at dawn, to rest,
but it doesn't, she wonders why, laughing.

*Let us be content each day
with the circumstances of our life.*

The geese at the reservoir fly at sunrise
without compunction, they have no use
for our presence, nor disuse. They choose
or are chosen by the light, and rise
over the dam to fly. Or does the ample
grass refuse them? The house of the earth
they had no part in making, no curtains
of dust to hang, no towels in the anterooms
they enter, and tuck their tails down to push
forth eggs they shadow from hot, unseasonal sun.

To rage against the cheek gone rough
the nap of the body hair, so soft once,
the risen flesh –

Curtains of lace I hang against light,
the palms against silk thread, the spider's web,
yes, even the Recluse my broom passes over . . .
House, my body, my boys.

Against concrete my soles press, complacent
in their rubber housing, the heat of yesterday's sun
radiant there. Yes, if the children – yours, or
any – were here to enter the household
take up their sneakers, bend their knees
to the sidewalk's warmth, tie up their own shoes . . .

My hands close on my own fingers. Today's sun
is hot, complacent in its house of sky.

Let us say no to the small child
who pulls at our earlobes, pats
the flesh of our inner arms, winds his fingers
like silk, his touch like silk
as he slithered from the house of our body.

Across from me she is writing
we are both writing and she is making
small sounds, she who is reticent, so tidy
and careful, so finely boned as we have been
walking and she listens and breathes
quietly. It is only now, yes, a catch
in her breathing that makes me look up, raise
my head to see her cheeks begin to shine
as she rubs her cheek. And still she is writing.

Can you tell me, please, what use
this weeping for what we both know is coming?

Said to Sarah, Ten

> And scribes wrote it all down.
> *Gilgamesh*

There is no one to say why
this face on the scrap of newsprint,
The *Times*, is not the face of my brother.
No one to say why her cat wastes
in a nest on the sofa, shawl and heating pad.
It yawns and gapes and whines
and arches its back.

How long will it last? she asks,
meaning grief, and I haven't the heart
to say a lifetime. Daughter.

Epistemology, I said in the dark
to her father, my head on his arm,
is my favorite subject, how we know what we know.

It will take so long, she says at intermission.
We hold each other in our common arms.
Mother and daughter, we are bound by mucus
and blood, the spilling of waters, flesh,
and the uses of smooth muscle.
I don't have the answer. It wasn't wisdom
brought her to life. I did nothing.
Now we sit in the dark watching
the orderly art of the body. Dancing.
People sweat in service.

I tell her in the dark,
when we're gone, when they're gone
under the earth, when all our names are forgotten,
this will continue, this dancing.

Fast Car on Nebraska I-80: Visiting Teacher

Early sun on fields.
A pheasant flushes and skims
the north ditch on air.
Students, I say out loud, rehearsing
in the car, *this morning*
our subject is nouns,
how to pin them down.
Gold is the color of freedom,
I say, *the fields Mennonites farm*
to yield more than an acre can.

Later, the most compelling noun
is *car*, fast skimming away from a class
I've asked to describe death
in terms of silk tatters, the smoking gun, for example,
of a brother shooting over his sister's head.

The girl in the front row
who daubed her eyelids purple
wrote about *the-one-who-is-gone*,
meaning her sister. And wrote
about *the-one-who-did-it*,
meaning her brother who shot the gun,
whom she ought to hate – and doesn't.

She doesn't. She misses the black hair
of his head, his brown eyes, her sister's
pale skin, now gone *dead-white*.
I don't make her read out loud.

First things they said, this is a Mennonite community
and a boy killed his sister here two weeks ago.
But they forgot to mention the family, other kids in school.

Early Monday, driving through wet air at seven
I'd noticed the horizon did a good job
on my heavy mind: what had seemed a knot
so snarled I couldn't get a nail in
began to unwind as I watched through the windscreen.

Here, the town is groomed, each stubble lawn smooth
in a yellow fallow. The houses are brick.
Each child in grades two through twelve
is clean and well-dressed. Some seniors
they tell me in class, drive Thunderbirds,
or go visit China in the summer. In the library
I have a glassed-in office usually reserved
for the Monday-Wednesday speech teacher.
I work undisturbed. Nowhere here
is violence I can see, only the peace of community.

Not here, or in the deep ditches where pheasant harbor
or the deer. Who couldn't be happy here?

Afternoon, with Cold

What's outside is summer.
What's inside is phlegm,
a foul effluvium rising
through lungs, gateway
air enters to dilute
miasmas, maybe environmental
illness – collective noun
for everything wrong,
the exterminator's spray,
chemical prods for growth,
hormones, the caustic
cleaners for tile, drains
all emptying into our
Ogallala aquifer –
some vision, magnifying
as my temperature rises
and all I have is a cold
in the head. Some
summer complaint.
That's all.

Sick

The third person I am
watches you bring tea to the iron table
rescued from the dump
put the knobby kettle steaming hard
by my arm.

I notice the porcelain cup
thin red stripe like blood
circling the rim your mouth
you bend to me peppermint
what's wrong tell me are you
dumb now stupid tell me where
you hurt? My mouth is stretched
over a rubber ball of fat. Everything
loud blurs your face inessential
dissolve you're gone and you know what?
I know nothing about you who are
body solid in its misery stupid melting
at every boundary it touches the hot
iron kettle the whole world we share.

Back

Jump, says the therapist
hold to the bars. Lean
backward, lean forward. Now
in sets of ten, early morning
late evening in the front room
working through the pain.

Light from Papa's body
light powdered his shoulders
light moved through bowing,
bowing, rocking, light
a burr language not to get close to
his child again closed out
the mystery of phylactaries
bound over freckles, the golden
hair of arms, muscles
and the black boxes on straps
packed with prayers at pulses
between the portals of his eyes
on lying down and on rising up,
brow smoothed by prayer, davening
before he goes fishing, my hand in his hand,
before reading, his body my cradle,
before walking, my head at his elbow,
before sleeping, my blank forehead under curls
useless, tangled, my empty portals. Pain.

Friday

Anyone possible to offend
I have. Today, spring out the window,
the flesh on my bones not clay
but firm over tibia, fibula,
the vertebrae of the back,
the particular small bones
of the feet, one of which you fractured
this winter, and the myriad
bracelets and chokers there
for the flenser/artist
who'd make jewelry of the dead.

Not today. "I'm putting out fires
with both hands," I explain
as I cancel lunch. I'm sorry,
I didn't do it right, you misunderstood,
forgive me, bless us all in our bumbles,
send me out to the brambles to dig
roots from the blackberry canes.
A regular whirling dervish of contrition
in the service of berries for us.

They're setting fire to the spring prairie,
you say, sitting down, drinking coffee.
Hello, you're welcome here in town
where sidewalks interrupt the weeds.
For the morning, so long as I don't speak,
you're enthralled. Have you heard the groovy one about . . .
And Mr. Downes turned his cauliflower ear to the crowd . . .
Certainly the fisherman caused a sensation when . . .
Before she died we escaped from the hospital and went to a
    movie . . .
How you know failure is when the birds on the roof . . .

What's next?
Make lists, hex the infamous,
perform rigorous examination of texts, scholarship.

I'm pooped. Friday's when the dead rise
on some scroll or parchment. Let us
consider the unrolling of ferns
in the supermarket trash amongst which
in the marsh of broken bottles
the blue muzzle of a tick hound
and the barrel of a magnum compete
for the color of slate. Dust
in the nose, pollen. Heat
between my shoulder blades

strokes wing buds as I bend over.
They're growing iridescent. But not yet? Not now?

> "The world is not something to look at; it is something to be in."
>
> Mark Rudman, Rider

I want my head to stop hurting
my heart to quiet. The light comes back,
ouch, more stimuli, on fire, needles.
I think of you in your high attic of words
a sudden salve. Nothing to explain, no shield
of paperthin skin between history and the untender world.
Every rush stilled.

Imagine buckets overflowing,
dear one, your warm hands plunged in.
Imagine children, their history and form.
And yours, the ones in folders, the ones forming
as the water swirls. Let me be in the world with you.
Let's walk, footsteps no sound on the river bank.
Let the calm dark lead us along, every muddy step a poultice
for our journey, our inquiry.

2. In verbs, as in
transboard, transearth,
transfashion, tranship,
trans-shape, transtime

Secrets

Teach me, they say,
the women with childbirth
three months behind them,
one with a dead baby and tears
the other come an hour down the highway
to find her car towed, her shirt front wet
with milk, and no money in her pocket.

Teach me, says Ruth, whose secret
is identity, pale face but she a blooded
Sioux. And Amy, muscular dystrophy,
who says no, you can't, when she doesn't
show up
for class.

Teach me, says the toe
leaking blood under the nail,
Teach me, says the rigid carapace,
solid, sealed on all sides
so the pulse amplifies, stirs
as currents of fire in the toe.

Teach me, babbles the darning needle
or the drill in its pan of water
burning over, settling on the stove.

And my job, to scald, bore, hold steady
under the light, the singe, the push,
the steady pressure, eyes open, the flash,
the bubble of blood,
the maroon gush, the icy relief.

Teach me, says the hole in the nail,
tiny, a door, and around it, rust, mold,
acrid release of what's sealed,
a tender probe to open, to hurt.

Heart Transplant

Here's the crowded restaurant
where we celebrate his return
to the law, marriage, friends.
His powder-blue-paper mask
puffs out and in with his voice
as he gives witness: First

a four-minute flat line on the monitor.
Then he's behind a crowd
of doctors and nurses around the bed,
then scalding light,
then the tunnel,
and then, he's surprised,
the outline of a human head
large, faceless, before him.

On my office bookshelf two miles away
a souvenir of my child's art class
a small head, smooth, blank face, head, neck, shoulders,
a clay bust – plus a delicate pile of interchangeable masks
each one thumbnail size. The head.

I listen like a Benedictine,
all ears for his words,
shaking, scared at once
by his absence
his unchanged presence
ruddy skin, blue eyes calm
over the luffing and filling mask
exactly their color and the hot sky.

He invokes the donor
a farmer across town killed suddenly
and cites his new passion for exercise and prayer

an hour's daily meditation as he mounts the treadmill.
Of course his wife is glad to have him back.

I gather this story in, ears cupped, torso bent
to the table edge between us. He reveals
his pain as the paddles struck, "greater than any,"
a gift of detail with lunch, for writer's hunger.

All night I toss and negotiate the pillows
for space, a cool place in the hot bed for floating,
trembling, afraid of good fortune and its wake.
The silence fills with the cat's long purr
and the steady heartbeat of my love and you
who sleep on for a while, thrown back into life.

Not for you the toxic chemicals, the hormones,
nor the surgeon's cuts to keep you up in the world
where the hunter's moon lights all our driveways with cobalt.

Footnotes

– for Burke Casari

1. The matter of shoes. Transsexuals have problems with size.

2. Wardrobe is a matter of taste, not gender.

3. As in, "If they don't know I pass muster. If they know they want to see my cock." Interview with subject 10/19/XX

4. The first question, "Does he have some kind of constructed penis?"

5. The problem of voice. His mother wondered if he had a cold for eighteen months? Esophageal cancer? This problem is representative.

6. A handwritten card dated two years before subject came out: "For Mom, who once said something about the difference between becoming an ornithologist and growing wings."

7. The mother's birthday was celebrated in increments, each one noted, every choice apparently made by considering other options. ". . . opening cards, breakfast out, cappuccino, choose two new books (Patricia Dunker's *Hallucinating Foucault* and Lisel Mueller's new and selected poems, *Alive Together*, the Pulitzer winner), a cherrywood picture frame, a new bud vase, ice cream cone dipped in chocolate, a salad for dinner, eight lobelia plants for the patio pots, four with white stars four purple-blue, phone calls to and from . . ." (cf. chapter 1, page 4).

8. "You will listen to me today and I will say everything I have to say, at once." Journal entry, quote from conversation.

9. Unpacking, phone messages, laundry, refusals, interest. But she had found an agent who liked the book.

10. Unopened Fosomax tabs with directions.

11. Her habit of walking out after dinner. His addiction to weight training for musculature. The sprained wrist.

12. Baci Perugina chocolate fortune: "One is alone with all the things he loves."

13. Bumpy weather traveling in a small plane.

Doing the Puzzle / Angry Voices

Pieces of prairie – the colors without names –
a tree of juncos, gray bellies rising, some song.

Prayers for the dead must praise God,
no mention of sorrow, no mention of death,
as if at the moment of inconsolable loss we might forget
　　to praise God.

The prairie we live on, what's underfoot plowed
to make a road we drive to the overpass –
eyes ache, what if I couldn't see the sun on Lespedesa, prickles,
but only a purple sheen on the black cardboard piece to reveal
　　its place in the whole.

Praise in the midst of disorder, so if the eyes roll back
　　in the china head, fall in,
and Marjorie is broken in my fifth year, praise Him.

Every book that documents birth
puts onto gender a meaning.
That piece of the junco tree is filled with sparrows.
The black is all color, no, the absence of color,
no engorgement at midnight, no purple.

On the puzzle board, what grows
is a picture of Adam and God
in collusion, all the beasts and no companion
to help. But still, if incorrectly,
each beast must be named.

In the office room I inhabit
a new lamp drapes light on
daily rituals of departure, a party I skip
to walk on new snow, granular, wool socks.

Here's narrow focus, patina, the coat of glass.
This piece: against a wedding feast, cranes at sunrise.
Every moment of night sleep, alert.

Praise at the keys   ivory, ebony.

We have to function twenty-four hours a day, seven days a week.
The responsibility of the body – catalogues coming through the
    mail, pages of photos, description, legends under color charts,
    alveoli, taste buds, hair follicles
so busy until the end, the rooftops – you, heart not only head.

Mother, each day of my life you raise your hand to touch me.
When he left me this time, my palm held the heat of his cheek.
Where does this piece belong? Who will tell me?

Prelude

We bring to our booth
pages packed full
of subject and verve
blood and tissue, the nutshells
of her history sharp under her elbow
as she leans hard, the full weight
of her language on this vision
or that one, and take in
the full length of our throats
swallowing, breathing air
we share with fifty others,
the smells of ripening toast
in the chrome slots, and we breathe out
tone, shading, the shouts necessary
for our Monday morning before light
streaks the sky, before the curtains close
against the glare for patrons in the next booth,
and the whole world opens . . .

For weeks, staticy news over the sink
as each night at the open refrigerator
I transport, unwrap, scrub, pare
and transform food for the family body.

Oh, Child-God who pushes
across the glass table top
the sharp clatter, the ruckus of our lives
blocks of Legos, steel gas tubes
torn across at the throat by some
torque from a machine too terrible
to posit now, at this table rinsed
by the kind and disinfectant cloth . . .

Trained by custom to serve
I set down the burden of dinner
wash my hands and begin to eat
the only possibility, finally,
turning away from the heat
reliable torque of hip socket
and ribs allowing the swivel
my body makes to sit down
or reach for the phone, gut
courage, to climb on the plane,

transfer, hoisting luggage
into the overhead bins, and arrive
at your side, child, in time
for your long surgery to come tomorrow
and I'll be there, your mother, where I belong
the old miracle of your birth belief enough
to see us through cut and clamp, the blood price
I signed to pay, and will, and will myself
onto the plane with books and cash, pastilles,
ribbons, cashmere socks, spare eyeglasses
and ribs, hip bones, reliable bone sockets, and
every recipe intact or documented, soft sacs bathed
reliable tongue tucked up into the silence broken
by only one word, love, one phrase, you can, one other,
I'm here, child, your absolute company
as you are changed – radically – from one thing to another.

Part Coquette, Part Monster

It's not clear precisely where she got that picture
of a different arm, which in the montage
becomes a giant phallus. But the impossible and
very funny result was . . . part coquette, part
monster, a parody of the cliche of woman as sex
object, elevated from a clever joke into art by the
elegant twist [she] gives to the ridiculous body.

Michael Kimmelman on Hannah Hock,
the German dadaist, New York Times

Mother and child, a montage of rage
and humor: Breast(s) the graceful center
of the installation: a rectangular panel
that twirls and quivers while the whole thing
        trembles
                continuously.
Cranes, a part of the high
backdrop, in the fields
like brown kites dropped, take off eventually
as solace; their wings unfold . . . silver hint
                of the Platte River at the right corner.

To pull yourself up by the teeth, clamp on the near bar, a standard
tube of metal, a chrome bit. Lift up over the shivering landscape
until you pop through, into vision, the blue void with clouds back-
lit O'Keefe entered and later, point fixed suddenly, a bone china
cup, the real thing, held up between your fingers and the window.
Oh, Lord, to surrender terror now abruptly, to lift free!

Trans

What do you care, she asked
at last, letting me get the good
from my hundred-dollar therapy time.
She's still your daughter. Whoops
she said going red all over the parts
I could see – face under permed hair
her neck chicken-wattled, even the top part
of her chest the V between her bowling shirt button
(marked JAKE on the pocket) showing blush.
I sobbed, quiet at first, swallowing salt
then louder wailing like some beached baby.

Son you mean, you old biddy, I croaked at last
crying a good ten bucks worth of earth time.
Who would have thought that little one
whose cheek turned away from my breast
would grow up HE. He started SHE,
a brilliant daughter.
                    It's the age, she said
not meaning puberty because he was long past,
thirty at his last birthday, but the times: everything
possible: hormones, surgery, way beyond unisex
jeans at the Mall, those cute flannel button-down shirts.

What will I do I whispered so deep into misery
I forgot she was listening and I was paying.
                    Afterwards on the bluffs at the heart
of the weirdest sunset since July 4th
I try to conjure his voice: "Mom
since sunup the sky's been dark but now we're talking
I see the sun come out perfect
for a walk and when we're through talking
I'm going out. Come with me?"
That voice: the same words and phrases, intonation

from me with his dad mixed in "like cake with too much
frosting," as my student said tonight in class. Be honest
here. Love is the word he said in closing. "I love you,
Mom." Transsexual – like life, not easy – in this century.
My kid. And me in the same boat with him, mine.

Transformation / Feathers / Train Travel

Meadow sun
on your shoulders
erases shadow
from behind the lens

I open the shutter.

In the photo, your hand is
a wing, feathers erupting
from your fingers.
You squint and smile, my hunk, my beauty.

The gorgeous Hulk's green skin
split reliably open his clothes each week
when the doctor he was
got angry, on TV. We both
loved the moment, Lou Ferrigno
in rags, entering the scene,
you prone on the shag grass
of our carpet, the kid,
me the mom with a plate
of warm brownies we expect to eat.

Now, twenty years later, on a train,
scanning your picture, I recreate
your "marvelous transformation,
not a particularly pleasant process
for the subject," said Nabokov
to his students. I'm one,
and still your mom as I travel upstate
trying to review your change
as the train sings to the waterfowl
landing and rising in the wetlands
we observe as backdrop, my thoughts

mired in "the tickle and urge . . . to shed
that tight dry skin, or die."

Nothing here is metaphor.

At the station you'll appear
as the guy I caught on film,
his fist filled with feathers.

In last night's dream you were my daughter
still an infant in arms, wrapped in a sheet
over a diaper, the only one I had.
"Relax," I said as we ascended the ramp
steep with cars or foot traffic around an invisible bend.

You tucked your small baby body close. Wind howled.
"We're two strong women," you said,
baby mouth damp with my milk. Of course I looked around
for someone to tell, my prodigy, as we crossed
the bridge safely and came again to the library,
or a bus, or the New York subway where we'll ride,
mother and son, home to breakfast.

In my dream where everything's metaphor
you're new, my new girl, and I'm studying
at a library table. Hours pass, a blank space
called flow, or I'm blank. The new guy comes
to take the desk, he's blank, slow, his truck
collection, metal miniatures reduced to two
he clunks on the oak to show me. Rushing
to leave, I lose my purse, my keys, my coat.
And now we're two, infant daughter and mom
chatting up friends I don't recognize, one
with a collection of clinky jewelry she pulls
from a lightweight purse suitable for travel,
another an expert on natural childbirth.
Lucky you're nursing, but baby, it's cold

outside and you're wet. The busman takes us on
wherever we're going and although this stop
is unfamiliar, I see the highway beyond
and across it, my office. And on and on.

"Though wonderful to watch,
transformation from larva to pupa or from pupa
to butterfly is not a particularly pleasant process
for the subject involved . . . he must shed
that tight skin, or die. As you have guessed,
under that skin, the armor of a pupa –
and how uncomfortable to wear one's skin
over one's armor – is already forming."
"You have noticed," Nabokov goes on,
"that the caterpillar is a *he*, the pupa an *it*,

and the butterfly a *she*." The great man
is winding down. The train is slowing.
And stops. And now we're here.
Of course the iron gates open on you.

Stone

Aaron picks up goose feathers
until his fist is crammed
with a fan of feathers
and me with the camera between us,
distraction from our constant talking.
I need to frame and document him
from a distance: his straight shoulders,
barrel chest, narrow waist, hips, muscular legs,
dark eyes, tanned skin, intense frown and laughter.
So male. Walking behind him and his brother
at the airport, their identical gaits, arms swinging
loose from their wide shoulders, Aaron thin as
Sarah never was, wearing his stepfather's outgrown jeans.

Angry voices: his learned gait. Learned muscles, learned grace,
handsome man wearing the Lucas water-snake bracelet
bought from his workbench at Old Oraibi, one unbroken curve
of silver Sarah wouldn't have worn, not even to try.
No, Mom I don't wear jewelry, nor the Hopi belt buckle either,
the one Aaron wears now every day. *Aaron is a handsome man,*
say my women friends. Very male. His arms are covered with
a dark silky hair. His legs are hairy and straight. Sarah wouldn't
wear shorts, not ever. Aaron, yes. He eats carefully, is lean.
Men are? he asks. *Women are? Tell me the story I don't know,* says Aaron.
The story about women. Tell me the story I don't know says his mother.
The story of your transformation.
How a girl child is male.
When I used to look in the mirror it was blank, says Aaron of Sarah.
And then Aaron says *Mom! I'm the same person.*
You're the one who had the sex change.
I've always been as I am. You bet.

My eyes see someone familiar, someone I love.
But where is Sarah whose chin rested on my shoulder?

My eyes are red, they fill again and again each day
as I listen to the news from the telephone, the radio, conversation.
I think a friend is dying, each day her face collapses a little,
yesterday her lips, pouty around her perfect teeth.
And my cancer writer needs a biopsy now, her CAT scan
a little shadow where last time there was none.
She goes out for groceries in the city heat wearing
a short, red dress, she's strutting her stuff. On the phone
we talk about sex. In the mirror my face is tired.

Another friend remembers us as mothers
with young children at Woody Park Pool:
Sarah at two in her striped one-piece,
her brother four, blue cotton trunks,
me in a French navy polka-dot bikini,
wet braid heavy on my shoulder as we bend
to splash with the kids in the shallow pool,
all of us soaked and warmed by the late sunshine,
the heat of the plains in high summer.

Today is twenty years later, ninety-some degrees
where I write with a friend before work.
This breeze is delicious my aunts would say
to each other in the forties, fanning their deep
bosoms before the hundred-degree heat sets in.
Train sounds, the trucks. We drink chocolate
to begin the day. My friend is to arrange
a repeat mammogram, a little something on the film to check.

My favorite piece from Aaron's new show,
a gray stone drilled off-center, the hole lined with silver,
dropped from a silver chain. I'll buy it if I can.

My friend says, *follow the pen.*
My dress becomes wings filled with wind,
a crosswind on the dock this early morning,
pebbles tossed as the tide comes in
over rocks in Maine, the sheen light drapes
at the cliff foot, the prickly wild roses and blackberry
bushes on the path, the smell of salt.

The camera is unashamed to be examining
the body of my child. We are not shy.
I look at his scars, less red, one less colloid.
His belly, his genitals, the pattern of hair on his torso.
He is plain, like Quaker rooms, tidy now and still beautiful.
Sarah overflowed like me. But in my bikini,
slim, muscular, flat-bellied, small-breasted.

(Aaron is glad to be rid of breasts. I look
in the mirror and see nothing familiar,
scars and absence, say it, one breast.)

Oh, love! All these words I've written before.
My pen is empty of words.
The wind fills my silk shirt by way of the sleeves,
stirs and opens my skirt.
The flow from the inner body, female, ample!

The mommy next to me on the dock lifts
her son into a small chair, unwraps his muffin,
pours juice. The wind picks up.

On this hot day I am chilly.
The doves at the white bird bath,
the crows at the copper
in our backyard, all will be thirsty.
They dip their beaks
into standing water and drink

40

in the hot early evening, dregs
fetid and scant, warm.

The child next to me lifts his cup,
sucks juice from the spout, fusses,
stretches his legs under the plastic table
which moves to accommodate him.
His mother steadies his cup.
The child chants his pre-language
accompaniment to the conversations of the aunts.
His name is Connor. *Connor, Connor!*
He runs to the edge of the concrete dock
carrying his stuffed puppy by the ears.
The longer I write, the smaller I grow
quiet in the rivulets of sound from the street.
If they toss me like the stone, I am content behind my camera
learning to point the lens, to look at the body of the world. *Click.*

No, cries Connor. No.

Why resist? In my dream I am unable to help, comprehend,
caught in weak flesh. My job is to pass on, distribute,
and as always, to witness.
Someone sees the cat with the flapping bluejay in her jaws,
says, *Leave her be. She's doing her job.*

Alive in the world, the chilled stone waits.

Before John and Maria's Wedding

In front of the throb
space opens in the skull,
space where the garden reassembles
without shrubs, golden yews flanking the gate,
pseudo-angels, the light at four, sword-like . . .

Instead, reassembling behind gauze
the thin time between now, over coffee, safe in company,
and flight – the airport, bus, and the blessing,
the exchange of rings, the lock sprung on the apartment
next door, your assault on the common wall
to make an extension, a tent, a shelter, a bond.

You, older son, will be married in the sight
of the company, blessed, and the common veil
of light will drape us all – great composer
and his wife, Elliott and Helen Carter, the assemblage
of blood – both sides – and the ancestors dead
on one side at the hands of the other, fled
from the scene – my mother who wouldn't leave
the car, not for anything, so her foot
wouldn't touch German soil your new wife springs from.

Time, thin fabric, the scrim Yawah plays behind,
bless our children, two in front
of this fleshly company, the other holding my hand.

The flesh will have to do now, this marriage
a healing you make for us, yourselves
who were never broken. Let our blessings
be sufficient here, the garden you move through
together, covered now by time and light.

3. In adjectives with the sense across, crossing or on the other side of

Historical Documents

– for John

Last night, dark windows, handwritten pages
in a binder on my lap
as I read again the story of your birth.
The papers turn easily as we labor, time moving
in a blur of day-after scribble, nothing
too bad, the dire predictions proved false
in coming years, and you here at last
in the same world we inhabit now waiting
for your child's birth. Son, you were the first time
I opened wide
for something wholly new.

My notes document vernix, the sheen of your scrunched face
fresh from my body, the length of your silence
in the delivery room. But

here, in the pages of the binder, my bald account
in simple language testifies to us both that birth
comes fast for the bearer, the child safely breathing,
the father, you, stunned by the dramatic head bursting
forth, safely standing by as the new child takes breath,
gives up its own first loud cry.

Fresh from the shower this morning, maybe the day
of her birth, I stand naked in my several scars, look,
and without thinking, reach for sky, stretch to hold
the supplicant's position, palms up to the sun,
stretched as far as I can
and breathe deeply in
a chant for Maria, who is your wife. Let her be safe
and wholly present, giving birth.

Mostly she is dazed now, talking on the telephone,
walking her miles, bathed in endorphins, vague

as she sort of remembers the camera's beep she turned off –
did she? how? The light in the bathroom is out
so she can't see what's happening, a mystery
she laughs, and your voice, son, going on about something,
my ears blocked, listening for your cry, the first cry
in this cold room where I delivered you to the world
we wait in for the birth of this child.

Where in myself is Victoria?
Where in myself is Hilda?
Where Samuel, where Dolly, Frank,
Aaron?
              The germ of the self thins
out like bells as the cathedral recedes,
a visit only, a ride through country green
with promise or golden death, white
ice on the road as the brougham skids
sideways, the people under the heavy lap rugs
shift, fall against each other and laugh,
adjust their caps and furs, remove
a mitten to tuck up the fallen braid of hair,
shake the linen handkerchief, bend to wipe
the child's nose who sits in front
next to his daddy, a Sunday ride,
the peace of the car concentrated in the fierce
blade of thin sunshine bisecting the space
askew into two compartments, one for the aunts
and grandmothers in back, the other, the space
where you ride through the world, child,
now dark now light as the landscape flickers,
the peal of bells fades to a cry
we know is coming.

Volunteers

Out the window, a kid-robin on a branch
shows me her size, the same as mama's
but fuzzy, an outline and then,
turning, her all-over splotches.

At the back of the yard, a blighted pine
shows a beige fringe in the emerald sumac,
they're big feeders, you've got to tend them
so everything else stays healthy.
That pine's dying from something. A storm?

On the radio, a story about customers
come to the clinic for mary jane,
$40 a dozen for marijuana cookies
or $80 an oz. for the best stuff
and the police won't close it down
because they'd have to cart us off
in ambulances! – a snort of laughter –
this one with lesions on his arms,
thin, and open sores and bruises.
Poor guy buys cookies as an appetite
stimulator. What would become of him?
What will become of me?

Dark letters, welcome! What a deal!
I'm gonna grab a cup of joe, java, and a cookie
before the gas guys come to cart off the old grill
we cooked hamburgs – upstate NY talk –
and hotdogs on. Flaky rusted now.
Here I am, happy and healthy, tip-tapping along
one minute at the time. Eating.

Even though I don't believe this mess is worth saving,
writing is like digging in clay the sumac plays out of,

black letters, the sound of Mom's voice, the crisp edge
of Papa's celluloid dresser set: buttonhook, shoehorn,
brush, mirror, comb, and what's that odd receptacle with the hole
for hair combings? To make jewelry? Papa bald as an egg.

He holds me, listening to the radio
night after every night, each night a story.
I wouldn't lie down without a headphone later
after surgery, a novel or poems for the heart.
Mama, read to me. Papa, I'm fuzzy, read me a story. Like that.
Or on paper. Like this. Tip. Tap.

Some Questions about the Storm

What's the bird ratio overhead?
Zero: zero. Maybe it's El Niño?

The storm, was it bad?
Here the worst ever. Every tree hurt.

Do you love trees?
Only the gingko, the fir, the birch.

Yours? Do you name your trees?
Who owns the trees? Who's talking?

You presume a dialogue. Me and you.
Yes. Your fingers tap. I'm listening.

Will you answer? Why mention trees?
When the weather turned rain into ice, the leaves failed.

So what? Every year leaves fail. The cycle. Birth to death.
In the night the sound of cannon, and death everywhere.

What did you see?
Next morning, roots against the glass.

Who's talking now and in familiar language? Get real.
What's real is the broken crown. The trunk shattered.

Was that storm worse than others?
Yes and no. The wind's torque twisted open the tree's tibia.

Fool. You're talking about vegetables. Do you love the patio
    tomato? The Christmas cactus?
Yes. And the magnolia on the roof, the felled crabapple, the topless
    spruce.

Lost Jewelry

My grandmother's diamond chip ring
set in filigree platinum, given to mark
my sixteenth birthday, a family gift
of transition. Carelessly removed
and returned to its box, dropped
into a suitcase I didn't lock
for a trip I took by air, on top.

My best friend's dead mother's watch
removed and dropped on the bedside table,
stolen by my boyfriend. Who else?

My first golden hoop – one of a pair
bought in Pharaoh's Jewelry Store, slipped
from my ear while swimming
in a friend's lake. NOT removed
for vanity when the bikini snapped shut,
sacrificed to that place of my greatest happiness.

My wedding ring – green gold filigree –
thrown from a moving car into perfect grass.

Lapis lazuli earrings torn from my lobes
by my own hands, dropped from a bridge
into icy water.

My grandmother's wedding ring
she flushed along with her spouse,
a family legacy that story,
now mine.

My second wedding ring, heavy
old 22k gold, irregularly beveled
by the jeweler's art, put off, unlucky,

to be cleansed by earth or flame
next generation, or sold. Now
hidden in velvet, eclipsed in darkness
in metal, behind locks, behind bars.

My birthday watch from Papa,
pink gold, tiny. "She's too young!"
cried Mom. I was. Gone.

The marcasite star on a silver chain.
I have it still. Fifty years. Don't I?

A double pearl ring from Daddy.
Which? The large or the small?
Same price. I'm fifteen. Shopping
together. The big one. The top
pearl cracks.

Mother-in-Law

In the nursing home you sit
in your wheelchair, fingers taped
together, hands in socks,
black cotton, marked with some guy's
name. Your head nods, you're a stranger
after twenty years, no teeth, no eye

glasses, no shoes. Our eyes
glitter on seeing you sitting
nodding among strangers
who are name-taped
to belongings, some guys
you don't know, one's socks

a mockery on your hands, socks!
Your son wipes his eyes
surreptitiously so I won't see, or the guys –
his brothers and nephew – sitting
nearby watching the TV duct-taped
to the wall against strangers

which is after all what we are, strangers
to you, your hands in socks
which at the wrists are taped
to your robe. I can't close my eyes
even though I'm sitting
away from the crowd with the only two guys

who are patients here. The other guys
are ours, my spouse and his kin, strangers
to their mom who is still sitting,
as she always will, in socks
not shoes, never gloves again, her eyes
blind without her glasses which are taped

so what, so what, taped
shut in her bureau. The guys
here in the home don't care if their eyes
weep in front of strangers.
They share their socks
and everything else on this floor, sitting

still on the floor, taped in, forever strangers.
They're all one of the guys in the chairs, sitting
still, their socks held forever in common. Sad eyes.

Women & Men

Women have babies, or can, or can decide not to
use the miraculous machinery.
Women walk downtown holding their daughters'
hands, or can if they're inclined,
each generation adding a link to the chain.
Women can work – or not – at the blessed
repetitive tasks of the body, cleansing
their flesh of the blood flow, a tender care
required – in whatever spirit – at regular intervals.
Women were girls, like boys, fast across
the meadow, diving into the pond
or carrying morning after morning the heavy buckets
of salt water caught up from the animal sea.
Blessed bone, ribs like his, flat brown belly,
small nipples, and the growing muscles of the shoulders
to lift . . .

Women, out for a walk, cross paths with men
holding red dogs on a leash, who strain and bark.
"Hi, Sweetie," calls a woman, smiling on the small
Irish setter, dropping down to dog height
at a distance. A man walks on, pulling the leash
taut against the straining dog. Smiles on the dog.
The woman walks on, slowing approaching the pair,
her palm turned outward toward the dog.
The man tugs, the dog skids on the twilight pavement
still hot from the day.
"He would jump on you," the man says.
"He'd love to jump on you."
The woman walks past, smiling.
"I'd be afraid," she says.
"I'd be very afraid."

Some Questions for the Evening Class

It is over already? Or have we just begun?
Janie writes an open door. Jason is revving up.

How did we start? Did light fill the window?
Did we begin in the dark? Pat has gone to Paris.

Holiday preparations begin. Opaque windows now.
We start to end. We leave each other stars.

What did you learn? Did you build a wooden dragon?
You said I'd stare at tundra. Denali walks in my eye.

How can I leave you all with your notebooks?
What will you write I can't read?

The year winds down warm still.
Remember the towed car? The coming surgery?
Stunned students? The cold wall?

Each one is writing now where we are. The rustling tree.
Still together here, free in this classroom. Will we remember
Chauna shaping a word axe? Mary Jane back from silence?

Insomnia III

He has a tumor in his brain
that much we know – and he's the father
of four children, the oldest fourteen.
Therefore this morning of sun so bright
we're asked to draw the shades,
let us praise the brain in its bone pan.

All night as I bow to the boom box
changing tapes, the electrical cord
between my ears carries a charge to respect,
adjust away from the fleshy thorax, over my head
to rest safely where it belongs, if it can be said to rest
anywhere naturally, on my skull.

                    O disordered
self, to require distraction all night,
stories poured in the porch ear –
for example, news of the man who counts the angel
residue of birds broken on our picture windows –
in order to obliterate the polite rustle
the possum makes with her babes
through the laundry yard to home
under the shed. And to miss at five
exactly, this spring season,
first bird song with first light . . .

                    O untrustworthy self
filled with appropriate terror of tumor
and broken wings, consider
flight, not the swollen plague tongue
in the sore mouth, but story.

Or the possum herself, laden, twentieth generation
of her family, in residence still in our yard,
how in spite of ghosts and grief
I know exactly – how? – her path
under the empty clothesline.

She

Organizing pneumonia is the diagnosis
for her lungs sick with emphysema. Rails
at her cortisone sentence for six weeks
hundreds of pills, a moon face, fatigue
under frantic energy, she is hard as nails
on the phone resisting all suggestions
attributing everything to the hospital
emergency room treatment for allergy
someone recommended – maybe I did.
I am hard as nails listening.

       This blessed morning
of midwinter spring after a full night
of stories on tape, good ones, I am still
hard as nails wrapped in cellophane
ready to put one booted foot after another
on the blessed ground, soft air, soft color sky,
soft skin lotion hands in parka flannel pockets
her sick lungs in my chest, emphysema,
packed and crinkling under my own flushed wings.

Letter from a Place I've Never Been

Where cold was supposed to be, the sun is warm.
You've promised no wind. The grass is calm
under the snow. The map showed the interior,
which is where I am. The trip was long. I knew it would be.

From the top of the earth, I saw no mountain,
though you promised, if the air was clear,
the mountain would show. But ribbons
of light swirled the vault of the sky.
The sun set at four. The sun rose at nine.

Moose and sled dogs, exotic creatures,
I'd thought to discover around some corner
or other by the salmon processing plant, never.
I'd brought my sunscreen for a tromp
through the woods. No woods. No trees.
Flat rock that seemed to be granite.

Alaska is as far from where I am tonight
as Chicago is from Seattle, where the layover
is long. Or, to put it another way, the way
of a friend, the distance from LA to NY,
a trip I've taken.

I'm scared of the cold, of the dark, of the journey,
the unfamiliar plants that perk into poems
I've read and reviewed. Some kind of weed,
not jewelweed from Robert Frost. Oh, why
did I say I'd travel? The tundra is something
strange like a sponge. And golden.

Not Now

It's not my turn
It's been my turn not
now under the hot shower
everyone safe for the nonce
even the old cat   no cancer
on her nose close to the brain
hoofing it into the spring evening
ice floe at the bottom of the driveway
even that one melting under the juniper hedge
the lilac flushing through its scale.

Summer

– for Aaron

This morning, up at six, waiting for
the flat white tablet embossed with a bone
to settle in my belly, I take up sharp scissors
and on clogs enter the raised beds to clip off
dead or dying flowers – various shades of deep purple
some with yellow throats, some lavender sports –
to gather a few full blossoms for the test tube
vase you bought me for my decade birthday.

The light flat against the old railroad ties
holding hard against earth, heavy clay overlaid
with wood chips . . .

Somewhere under the chenille robe, behind
the long zipper and the scars, is the young girl
packing for camp. White shorts and Ts
for the Sabbath, candlelight to welcome
a day of rest – reading on bunks, bare feet
rubbing the scratchy wool blankets.

What does that girl know about dying
or illness, AIDS, the cancer in the brain? How,
as she lifts the toad free of pond moss,
hot fingers carefully moving over the smooth skin,
to thumb a wedge against the cool suck, can
she touch her power to watch over the world, live
here touching tenderly with passion, teach
the scarred woman sitting in early light
deadheading the flowers, teach her to watch?

Surely I didn't intend to confront
anything more this season of planting
than the hired work I do – reading manuscript

texts for Longman, diddling through writing a book
with my transsexual son, in good company,
filling the patio pots. My tragedies already
suffered, transformed, and put between covers.

Better the inquiry into the nature of ticks
their habits, their prodigious swelling
without bursting, bodies thick with life,
scurrying, detached without host, to another.

Anna Maria Is Coming, or Maybe Thomas Barton, or Max!

New life! Will he toe out like Dolly, like John? Will her eyes be
    fires?
Blue and green, like Papa's, the ocean at the shore?
Will she sing in the bath? Play piano in her diapers?
Will her heart leap at large machinery? Will he say, "Dribe,
    dribe,"
to his daddy, entering the tunnel? Will his hair be red? Will her
    hair curl?
Will her little face have the circumflex eyebrows of her mother?
    The pointed chin?
Her hair be fair, bright blonde? Will she frown at the light by the
    river?
Oh, let her head fill with Greek Owls, her mouth with honey
    wine.
Let his hands cup the keys, the air of the studio filling with
    sound, the crunch of
cornflakes, the sift of raw sugar on the tongue, the great chords.

And let the parents be fierce forever, Lord, as You are, exacting
price and penalty for Your gifts, so they grow strong and joyous,
blessed by the memory of the black car, open to air,
chosen by a child in token of the power they give over,
their lives in service to new life, the great melt of petals under
    snow, the green rising.

4. With the sense beyond,
   surpassing,
   transcending

Hello

my best shoehorn, my malachite pillow, my tulip of chocolate, my shoelaced rib, my waterfall below the kitchen, my dark pressure, my icy back of the neck migraine specific, my castle in the birdbath, my supreme coffee grinder, my ice cream refusal, my airplane crash, my bottle rocket exploding leaves in the gutter, my no-you-don't thermos thrower, my gummy bear licorice eyelash, my mountain of glass slippers melting into tropical punch, my stars, my neon, my bonefire, my passion.

The Address on the Map

Rosemont Crescent
179 the address where my confirmation
class meets each Thursday. "As in Genesis,"
says Mrs. Levi, "the woman from the man's rib."
Mrs. Levi is Selma, she drives a convertible,
sling-backs and mules, not like Mom or her sisters,
in cotton housedresses, who don't drive.
She lists the false Messiahs, Zabatti Zevi, the others,
to explain smart men with grand but wrong ideas
like Mr. Levi, I think, who worked in the yard
Monday through Friday and did the cooking.
Mrs. Levi has ideas, and glasses with rhinestones,
that book, The Fall of the Temple, and History,
and she invites George, the handyman who bikes
into our neighborhood to put up the screens, take down
the storm windows, whooshes out his false teeth
to scare us, into her kitchen for tea over ice
then sits down to talk, her pink mule hanging
from her painted big toe dripping feathers.

Wonder Woman's Rules of the Road

1. The wall? Walk around. Your legs work, don't they?

2. Wear armor at vulnerable sites. Perfume at pulse points?
   Better, silver bracelets.

3. Learn from heros: tools extend range.

4. The best asset is a wise mother, better a goddess.

5. Absent a mom, girlfriends, comrades.

6. Bind loose hair with a fillet. Keep your face exposed.

7. Anger is power.
   Justice is power.
   Make laws when laws don't suffice (*Herland*)

8. Stand with legs apart: a triangle is more stable than a stick.

9. Avoid camouflage.

10. Don't tangle your legs in a cape.

11. Strong abs are to die for.

Wonder Woman's Bracelets

Do they cover scars, a suicide attempt? Self-mutilation? Cigarette burns, tiny cuts, gauze and band-aids? In the 60s, you bet. Those mad girls who wrote. Controlled hysteria. Let loose. Therapy. My jewelry box, top left drawer. A trio of silver cuffs (one a spare). The water serpent belongs now to him. (Him?) You.

In the 50s, they were armor. Underneath, perfume at pulses, why? The flutter to waft scent to the boys. I lift my wrist in chemistry class, breathe in. The naked wrist.

Clamp-on bracelets so veins, those incipient geysers, hide. The closed and vulnerable wrists flash like shoulder points under iodine-oil at the beach. In sand, sun, and waves, all flash and movement. Never take them off. What's underneath's taboo.

Wonder Woman and the Disrupted Body

Imagine Wonder Woman with one breast. Draw her costume. Alter the top. Only one bracelet. Is it wider? The wooden boot.

Wonder Woman's Rules of the Road — 1962

1. Watch your wrists. Cut, they're geysers: sexual, lethal.
   Decorate all death sites, pleasure points: earlobes, throat,
   labia, lips, elbows, wris. . .t(s) with scent.

2. Your inner arms, thin and veiny. Perfume daubs won't save
   you. Silver bands, wide at both wrists, may. They deflect your
   own gestures, others.

3. Flaunt your belly if it's flat, muscled. Abs are to die for.

4. Stretches every day; don't forget the shoulders. Bounce light
   from the chin, collarbone, especially in motion. Be in mo-
   tion. Bounce _____ from the wrists.

5. Those headaches? Nothing but a slipped halo, a fillet binding
   your forehead, a princess crown.

6. Brunettes have more choices.

7. Learn the uses of tools: a whip, a lightening bolt: watch and
   learn.

8. Flaunt your legs. They work, don't they?

9. Boots, always.

10. Tampons don't show at the beach.

11. Your legs work, don't they?

Wonder Woman's Costume and Address

How come she gets to wear her swimsuit in the city? How come her boots don't wrinkle? How come her top and bottom don't match? How come she gets to wear earrings with her leotard? How come she doesn't have to wear glasses? How come red, white, and blue isn't tasteless? How come she doesn't have to wear stockings? How come her lipstick's Fire & Ice? How come she lives with girls on an island? Is there an island of girls? Show some respect!

Wonder Woman and Daughters

She didn't have one, but she could've.

Aaron at Work / Rain

By the light box propped in the window,
bare chested, scars rosy in artificial sun,
he crouches over his workbench.
Dental tools in their holder at hand, silver discs,
his torch, the tiny saw. Light flares, breaks on
his earring as he turns his head,
frowns, dark eyebrows almost meeting.
He takes a watch from his jeans pocket,
rubs it absently over his beard, electricity.
The braid clinks its beads as his head
turns, reading something. Now he rises, goes
to the cupboard, mixes wallpaper paste with water.
The pile of miraculous papers, shot metal
threaded with linen, he sorts to start
a papier-mâché hypodermic needle he's building on the table,
matches to the real one he used this morning,
adds it as a detail to the mask to change the meaning:
a revolution: what he's about. Out the window the black car
beads up rain. He never drives it. An emblem, but of what?
A memory of pain, his slouching walk just home from hospital?
Where is the child whose shoes I bought? Where the bread
we kneaded? Where our kitchen? Our dead?

Sarah Returned to Me, Wearing the Poet's Gloves

Her capable hands hang down,
covered in cashmere, between her knees
like a man's, the gloves the only interruption
in the field under the seminar table where my students
argue the merits of poems and the visiting poet.

The gloves were black, loose at the wrists – an expensive style
made in a postcolonial factory – and smelled of Ma Griffe,
which she raised to her face to inhale now and then.
The flower skin of her cheeks shone in overhead light.

Along with the gloves, she was wearing
a peach jacket of silk, loose at the waist, loaned
by Elizabeth Taylor, a colloid ribbon from Adam's apple
to collarbone. Sarah had been changed.
Yet she was the same.

What will you do with your extensive surgery? I asked.
Who cares, she said, smoothing her hands over her chest,
fashionably flat. Her abs below kapok shoulder pads
inverted a perfect triangle, like page 24, *Vogue*.
The cashmere gloves crackled on silk.

Where I had been wedged, between an Indonesian cushion,
tufted in triangles, and a feather pillow, space developed.
Light deepened to stone. My eyes failed. In my ears,
the cannon crack of trees exploding one after another.
Yet Sarah was with me, our hands clasped.
The cashmere gloves left by the poet warmed my palm,
kept Sarah safe from cold skin. We walked
through the residue of the world, hand in hand, calm.

Company / 3 A.M.

The cold kitchen, the cat circling my feet for warmth,
nothing properly in place or tidy, surely you wouldn't
be sitting here with me – no fit place to entertain
your sprawl of words, to drape your scarf – yet
here you are. The Hubble telescope is newly fixed
and clicking its news. Your pen tracks it, opens
a space on the page for the contraption of stars,
those tall, membranous chambers we saw on the news.

You are welcome here, imagined in so much detail.
So I put up the kettle for our second cut of tea,
the chunky raw sugar cubes, the vat of honey.
And look, I say, the new life your daughter begins
spirals right out of the girl you've been,
down to his thready eyelashes, the new moon fingernails.
That girl you were who took her belly home
made clear to her folks the need for layette.
You stitched the gowns, shifts, chose diapers, the pins,
even the belly binder you never used.
The same spiral star nursery the Hubble showed
ties her to you and you to him, this new child forming.

> And how glad I am to listen
> to the kettle begin its rattle,
> its billow, its sputter, its hot gush
> from the spout as I sit here
> writing with you in the kitchen, where else.
> 3 A.M., a good time for birth, eh, friend?

The cat on my lap begins her rumble,
the overhead light caresses the crystal
brainhead paperweight, the refrigerator
cycles on, all pulses and frail light
from the door opening, and I'm feeling better,

my pen extending its line clearly enough
for me to follow, the sugar cube in the cup
dissolving the sour while out the window to the east
surely light is trembling at the edge of the horizon.

Now if I could believe my own heart clenched
as raw sugar and the caramel-freckle-brown
color I love, the news I carry scalding enough
to melt it . . .
          only a hot tub filling slowly as light breaks
over my knees, thighs (they opened for you, child,
you didn't need to ask!), my belly, my ribs,
steam climbing over my heart turned syrup . . .
then I could lift, embrace my daughter
as he is, changed, turned right around,
all expectations sloughed off, child,
you are risen, new again, from the sweet
bath of your mother's heart.

First, Thus

The title refers to a designation used when
pricing books: not the first time in print but
the first in this particular edition.

Darkhead pushdown long, so small
tall otherman playing stardust melodies
fractured into waves so high apart
recombined into soothe and measure,
as in birdcry out the window, drowse
between every pain so pronounced
in one locus, only here he is,
as promised, love, love,
love out the window, see what
we've made come visit.

Elbows ache to hold, that's the plain truth,
so whatever else you've got to say, say this:
fingers were made to touch fingers. Open the light
up and tune up the corners, this lad's
jumping and another beside him. So grin!

Blessings in crackling thick
hair tied into clumps, dyed fluorescence who shaves
between or wraps string packages over waves
so harsh they jump the ears to crumbs get out
gotta get out recombine listen here, the idea
you've got is the idea's endtwist, mine twists
around both and Voila! here's visitors.
How long the stay?

One by one over land and sea, in air
they came, tied by thread together, o matter twisting
glistening red causation, no never mind the thrush
somewhere sings whether brown thrasher
or varied in that city oil ooze person to person
and the beast sits on our laps so long we crouch
down. Push, s/he said and someone did. Welcome, son.

The Storehouse

For once we add to the measure
the storehouse keeps safe,
not come in the night
with burlap to probe the grain,
diminish the golden hills. For now I know
the phone pulse at two brings
news of a comet, look up.

Your garden voice deeper for sure
but you, for all we've been through,
are identical genetically to the daughter you were,
your locutions your steady fingers on the trowel.

Yaweh, eternal, forever at play in the universe,
jester, let me stay last in line as I am now.

Early Morning, Left-Handed

Lear's five *nevers* over,
the fool hanged, and Cordelia
and Lear dead at last, Edmund
reported and yes he was loved
by both evil sisters, so what.
I'm awake in the dawn. Cold
stone floors. The cat. His
father loved him too, I tell
my son on the phone, my
son just married. Let him
cleave to his wife. Let my
old flesh resume its boundaries,
let go. No divisions of the kingdom.
Will they write of my courage
killing the snake? We know
the dreamy answer to that one.
Honey tea swirls us sweet;
never fear the village fair,
lights stay on all night.
Tea bags bottomless coffee
cup. Ashes in the grate sweeten
the garden provender. Clay.
Ripeness is all. The fool lives on,
my left elbow's cartilage feather.

Visitation: Pink Foam Letter

Under the seat directly in front
a child's alphabet letter

Under my heavy briefcase
a new texture, sponge

On the wet tarmac waving
adult child, son.

Here thirty thousand feet straight up.

After four years trying,
scars flat, waving
my son, a fine visit.

Now forever as I travel
the pink S my company.

The Funeral of X, Who Was Y's Mother

This woman who died last night in her daughter's arms
saying thank you, to whom? God for the easy death
called The Kiss, which the Rabbi tells us is God's blessing,
the touch of His lips to forehead that withdraws the divine
spark, life, from the body? Or thank you to her daughter,
most blessed by this witness, who wonders aloud which
meaning, a question in my ear as I bend down to her.
You deserve thanks, I say, either way. And we laugh
at the courtesy of her mother, who died during spring break
"so I shouldn't have to miss classes."

Shakkinah, the holy part of God that is Woman,
we are told, so a child, the Rabbi says, leapt to his feet
at her footsteps in order to honor the divine spirit
within her. He grew to be honored, but this mother,
"her price was above precious gems."

She was one of six surviving children
of parents who had "left behind in Europe ten others,"
no reason given, but we know, counting the years
backward. Will it never leave us, this grief particular
as sand we are told to brush off after the whirlwind
abates? Each grain in the eye moves and scratches
as I search the bowl of sky horizon to horizon
for a sign of the lost. Each particular ash invisible

as she is within the daughter who remains with me,
in my arms, bent for news whispered with deep delight
that the final gift a parent gives, to die in a child's arms,
is enough. We laugh and cry at once, which is seemly,
while the Mother of us all cries out and laughs, One
part at best, and holds me as I bend to myself to discover

not what I can't hope to understand – that which
we are enjoined not to worry – fondle, turn over
and over – but some small way into the magnificence,
abundant and ever moving, of the breathing and continuing
flesh.

Acknowledgments

Thanks to the following magazines and books in which these poems first appeared, sometimes in slightly different form:

Atlanta Review: "She"

Connecticut Review: "First, Thus," "John and Maria's Wedding," "Historical Documents," "Prelude," and "Early Morning, Left Handed"

The Extraordinary Tide: New Poems by American Women, ed. Erin Belieu and Susan Aizenberg (New York: Columbia University Press): "Volunteers," "Before John and Maria's Wedding," and "Fast Car on Nebraska I–80"

Kunapipi: "Insomnia III," "Trans," "Aaron at Work/Rain," "Every Way," and "Anna Maria Is Coming, or Maybe Thomas Barton, or Max!"

Nebraska Review: "Fast Car on Nebraska I–80: Visiting Teacher" and "Avoidance"

The Plains Sense of Things: Eight Poets, ed. Mark Sanders (Grand Island, Nebr.: Sandhills Press): "Drought: Benedict, Nebraska" and "Fast Car on Nebraska I–80: Visiting Teacher"

Pleiades: "Women & Men"

Poetryetc2 and *Catalyst 2:* "First, Thus" and "Aaron at Work/Rain."

Rattle: "Sick"

Sundog: The Southeast Review: "Heart Transplant"

Warm thanks to Jonathan Holden, Robin Becker, Aaron Link, Constance Merritt, Suzanna Tamminen, and Marge Saiser for close readings and advice about this book, to Dika Eckersley for design and friendship in all my projects, and to LeAnn Messing as always for manuscript and personal support. Dawn Elliot and Dale Nordyke have been with Aaron and me through these changes. They are our family, which also includes Jeff Raz, Sherry Sherman, Micah Sherman Raz, Amelie and Abigail Raz, Jennifer Lenway, John Link, Maria Schoenhammer, Anna Maria Schoenhammer Link, Eva Maria Schoenhammer Link, Vera Spohr Cohen, and Jennifer Susan Cohen. We remember Jonathan Alan Raz (1955– 2000) with love. Aaron Link chose the order of the poems.

"The Funeral of X, Who Was Y's Mother" was written in memory of Tilly Dann Geffen (1910–1995).

Library of Congress Cataloging-in-Publication Data

Raz, Hilda

Trans / Hilda Raz.

p. cm.

ISBN 0-8195-6503-2 (cloth : alk. paper) –

ISBN 0-8195-6504-0 (pbk. : alk. paper)

1. Transsexuals–Poetry. 2. Gender identity–Poetry.

3. Mother and child–Poetry. I. Title.

PS3568.A97 T7 2001

811'.54–dc21   2001026556